Days Out Around Naples

Gillian Birch

Cover Photo: Naples Pier Credit R. Birch

ISBN-10: 1517775361

ISBN-13: 978-1517775360

Marjory Stoneman Douglas

There are no other Everglades in the world. They are, they have always been, one of the unique regions of the earth; remote, never wholly known. Nothing anywhere else is like them: their vast glittering openness... a river of grass. May it always be so.

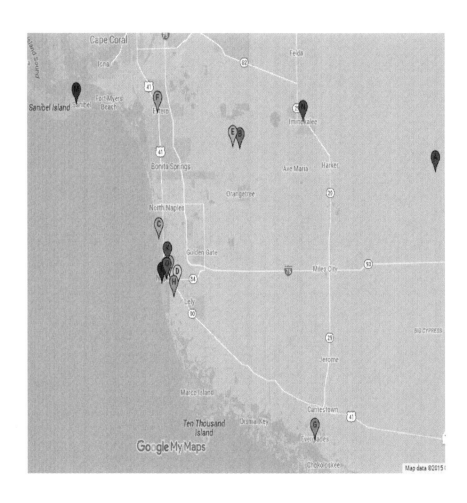

Key

- Billie Swamp Safari
- Bird Gardens of Naples
- Clam Pass Beach & B'walk
- Collier County Museum
- Corkscrew SwampSanctuary
- Koreshan State Historic Site
- Museum of the Everglades
- Naples Botanical Garden
- Naples Depot Museum
- Segway Tour of Naples
- Naples Zoo & Gardens
- Norris Gardens
- Sanibel & Captiva Islands
- Scenic Drive to Immokalee
- **Tin City**

Contents

An Introduction to Naples

Like much of Florida, Naples had little to attract tourists just 100 years ago. Virgin forests, cypress swamps and a stunning stretch of sugar-white sand marked what is now a most desirable city for residents, snowbirds and international tourists.

The first street to be developed in Naples was Gulf Street and it ran beside the beach which at that time was 100 feet wide. Both the beach and Gulf Street have since fallen victim to erosion. Naples oldest house was at 60 12th Avenue South and was built in1886 by John S. William. It was later occupied by six generations of the founding Haldeman family before sadly being lost to development.

Naples Hotel and Early Development

Early tourism began in 1889 with the building of the Naples Hotel, built by Kentucky native and visionary, Walter Haldeman. The hotel became the social hub of the growing community at that time and the food it served was legendary.

The 600-foot pier was also built by Haldeman in 1891, along with the first Post Office on the quayside. The pier was used to unload building materials from the steamboats which were the only means of transport at that time. It also served the town's early visitors and their luggage, which was hauled to the hotel along a wooden boardwalk.

Haldeman also built Palm Cottage, now the home of the Naples Historical Society HQ and the city's oldest surviving home. It was pressed into service as overflow accommodation for guests when the Naples Hotel was full. Such was the hospitality and success of this hotel outpost that by 1916 a 40-room annex had been built along with The Inn which stood on the corner of 13th Avenue South and Gordon Drive.

Naples' first school was built at 151 Broad Street South in 1905. The single-room schoolhouse had one teacher who taught all grades. As the town and school expanded, a second school was built in 1920 on Fourth Street South, between 10th and 11th Avenues. When this was replaced by a new school on Third Avenue South (now the Gulfview Middle School) the Fourth Street building was divided into four residences which can still be seen.

It was not until 1919 that the first grocery store opened on Third Street South and is still part of the downtown community. The same year, Naples' first golf course opened between Fifth and Eighth Avenues South and Third/Eight Street. Primitive by today's standards, golfers had to make their own tees using wet sand as there were no wooden tees at that time. This downtown golf club was superseded in the 1930s by the new Golf Club and Beach Club Hotel on the oceanfront, which remains a luxury resort today.

The grocery store was followed in 1927 by Ed Frank opening Naples' first garage, after filling in a huge gator hole on the corner of 11th Street South and Tamiami Trail. Ed loved tinkering with mechanics and built several Swamp Buggies to go hunting in the Everglades. The original prototype "Skeeter" vehicle, which was built from a junk Model T Ford with an orange crate seat, has since been restored and is now part of the Collier County Museum. Later models of Ed's swamp buggies were used for racing and always took part in the annual Swamp Buggy Parade. A surviving 1941 "Tumble Bug" can be seen at close quarters at the Naples Depot Museum.

Rail and Road Connections

The Tamiami Trail was a major feat of construction connecting Tampa with Miami, hence its name. It finally opened in 1928 and the incredible story is told on display boards at the delightful Museum of the Everglades in the old laundry in Everglades City. Part of that story includes how the construction of the trail was underwritten and supervised by local businessman Barron Collier, who was later honored by having the newly formed county named after him.

Although the Tamiami Trail made Naples far more accessible, a greater impact was the arrival of the railway in early 1927. The Orange Blossom Special arrived at the Seaboard Air Line Railway Depot in a cloud of steam and a blaze of publicity.

Life continued in Naples in a pleasant but far-from-easy manner due to the heat, mosquitos and other hardships. Much of it is recorded in a Prohibition-era movie entitled *Naples on the Gulp* by Naples' resident doctor Earl Baum. He lived in Palm Cottage with his wife Agnes from 1927 and they frequently hosted social evenings with screenings of the film, much to the delight of their family, friends and neighbors.

One unusual occurrence to break the predictable routine of life in Naples was the beaching of 20 whales on the beach in1933 and a further tragic suicide of 69 blackfish whales two years later.

Thomas Edison, Henry Ford and Harvey Firestone were known to be regular visitors to Naples from their winter estates in Fort Myers – another fascinating place to visit. Photographs of their picnics, camping, hunting and fishing expeditions with early Ford motors can be seen at the Edison-Ford Winter Estates Museum and decorating the walls of the Bass Pro Shop in the Gulf Coast Town Center Mall in Estero.

Naples Real Estate Pioneers

The explosive growth of Naples can best be charted by its telephone exchange. In 1947 the city had 142 telephones; 89 for residents and 53 for businesses. Today the city has over 20,000 residents and more than 17,000 homes.

Early developers recognizing Naples' potential were Forrest Walker and his sons Lorenzo and Robert. They developed the prestigious Aqualane Shores which now has multi-million dollar properties on the prime waterfront estate location. They opened the project in 1950 with a barbecue and gopher tortoise race, such was the limit of their early marketing budget! They also established the First National Bank of Naples and Lorenzo served on the Board of County Commissioners from 1950-56.

At much the same time, Port Royal was being developed by Glen Sample who had made his money in radio advertising. His marketing was in a total different style to the Walkers, producing glossy magazines featuring luxury homes at Port Royal with a luxury yacht moored at the end of the garden and a Silver Cloud Rolls Royce on the drive. Sales were slow in the late 1950s and 1960s but he held firm to his advertising slogan that "There'll never be another Port Royal" and time has proved him right.

Fame arrived in Naples in 1951 in the form of the cast and crew of the Warner Bros film *Distant Drums*, including the heartthrob actor Gary Cooper. The movie later premiered at the Naples Theater and the whole city was there to see it. This put Naples firmly on the map, and the city embraced the inevitable growth and development that followed.

In 1960, the 160 mph winds of Hurricane Donna brought devastation and huge change to the area. The county seat was moved from Everglades City, which was too remote and vulnerable to continue as the Collier County hub. The obvious choice was Naples, by then a flourishing city which was going from strength to strength.

Modern-day Naples Attractions

One enduring Naples landmark is the huge banyan tree that stands in the garden of Palm Cottage. Said to have been planted by Norman Prentice Sloan on his arrival in 1916, it has certainly witnessed remarkable changes over the decades. Today, a tour of Palm Cottage and the adjoining Norris Gardens introduces visitors to Naples' early history, told through the eccentric characters and historic buildings of this unique city.

Palm Cottage has had several names reflecting its multiple changes of ownership and use. Perhaps best remembered are Alexandra and Laurence Brown, who bought the spacious cottage (at that time known as the Hamilton Ontario house) for $8,000 in 1944. Their legendary cocktail parties, announced by them hoisting a flag, and their eccentric lifestyle with their basenji hunting dogs and vintage Mercedes coupe are all part of Naples' colorful history. In 1979 the Naples Historical Society bought Palm Cottage from the Brown estate. Now fully restored, this oldest surviving home is listed on the National Register of Historical Places and is one of the city's most popular attractions.

A visit to the Naples Depot Museum introduces more of these enterprising early settlers, including characters such as Speed Menefee who was pressed into service as the city's first mayor in 1925. After being sworn in and making a speech, he promptly resigned and became known as "The Fifteen Minute Mayor".

Browse the galleries, boutiques and shops on Third Street South, dine al fresco at some of the wonderful restaurants on Fifth Avenue South or relax on the beach and enjoy this unique and prosperous city. When you fancy taking a scenic drive, delving into Naples' history, getting out on the water, visiting Naples Zoo, exploring the Botanical Gardens or visiting Naples Bird Gardens, *Days Out Around Naples* has everything you need to fully enjoy the plethora of attractions that now surround this fascinating southwest Florida city.

Happy trails!

What's What

Introduction: Each chapter begins with a short description of the attraction and what it offers, to help you choose a day out to best suit your needs.

Location: Full address, contact details and location make getting there very easy.

What to Expect: This section gives a full and detailed description of what the attraction has to offer, including guided tours, personal tips, best times to visit and other information for you to get the most from your visit.

Where to Eat: These are all family-friendly places that I have personally experienced and would happily go back to. The businesses did not know I was gathering information for a book; I was simply there as an ordinary paying customer.

Cost: Admission prices and cost of boat trips, guided tours etc. are all correct at time of going to press in 2015. They are intended as a guideline only and may change.

Opening Times: I have supplied general information, telephone numbers and website links. It is advisable to call and confirm details before setting off, to avoid disappointment.

Nearby Attractions: Once you have enjoyed visiting your chosen destination, other nearby attractions are suggested to extend your day out or include as a detour on your journey home.

Billie Swamp Safari

Che-hun-ta-mo! (Hello!) from the Seminole Indians at Billie Swamp Safari. This authentic eco-attraction is set on 2,200 acres of untamed Florida Everglades. Located within the Big Cypress Seminole Indian Reservation, it is the largest of the five Seminole reservations in the state. A visit to the attraction offers the chance to see a wide range of Florida wildlife, visit an authentic Seminole encampment and meet members of the Seminole tribe who live and work on the reservation. You can even stay overnight in one of the rustic Chickees lining the airboat trail, and who knows what you will see and hear!

A day at Billie Swamp Safari is far more than just another airboat ride. The attraction includes wildlife exhibits, a

Swamp Buggy Eco-Tour, airboat tours through cypress domes, alligator feeding and excellent Snake and Critter Shows. See Rangers handling all types of exotic wildlife and dine on alligator tail, frog legs or more orthodox fare in the Swamp Water Café.

Location
Located on Hwy 833 off I-75 between Fort Lauderdale and Naples.

30000 Gator Tail Trail
Clewiston
FL33440
Tel: (800) 949-6101 or (863) 983-6101

http://www.billieswamp.com/

Things to Do at Billie Swamp Safari
The drive to Billie Swamp Safari takes in plenty of farmland and flat prairie along the edge of the Everglades as Hwy 833 winds its way from I-75 northwards through the scenic Big Cypress National Preserve.

On arrival, park in the marked area and explore the animal exhibits, huts and wildlife that are located on the edge of the flowing river. Tickets and maps are available from the Welcome Center and offer single attractions or an all-inclusive pass which includes an airboat ride, a swamp buggy eco tour and the chance to attend all the live animal shows, making the pass particularly good value for money. Keep a check on the timetable as you enjoy the day so you don't miss the Critter Shows and the Alligator Feeding at the Gator Pit, which has stadium seating.

The airboat rides are on a first-come, first served basis from the dock and times are posted for the next airboat ride, so waiting is generally not necessary. The airboats hold 8-10 passengers and riders are given earplugs before boarding. The rides certainly live up to the sign on the dock promising: "It is noisy and you will get wet!" The 20-minute ride is fast and exciting with plenty to see. However it is not a nature safari with a commentary – that comes with the Swamp Buggy Tour.

The airboat sets off along the trail through reeds and grasses and past the authentic native Chickee huts on the riverbanks. The water is fairly clear and shallow and the area is teeming with herons, limpkins, osprey, anhingas, vultures, fish and alligators swimming or basking on the banks.

The ride goes slowly through a forest of ancient moss-draped cypress trees with their protruding knees and it is very still and eerie. However it is a good opportunity to spot all sorts of wildlife in their native environment. The Seminole tribe has some unusual animals to see along the trip so don't be surprised to spot water buffalo, bison, wild boars, red African deer and even ostriches as you enjoy the ride through the wetlands. There is also the sign of the Six Tribes on the hillside and a statue of an Indian Head honoring Chief Billie to look out for on your airboat ride.

After all that excitement you may want to explore the animal exhibits which include a rare Florida panther.

Alternatively, take a stroll along the boardwalk while waiting for the next ride on the swamp buggy. These big-wheel vehicles carry passengers high above the wet prairie edge of the Everglades, giving great views of Florida wildlife and an authentic Seminole encampment. The guide points out wildlife, offers a commentary and is extremely knowledgeable about the Florida Everglades, so feel free to ask questions.

Various shows take place at set times throughout the day and they are extremely informative and well-presented by one of the Park Rangers. The shows are suitable for all ages, from young children to adults as everyone will be fascinated by the procession of animals that the Ranger presents. All the audience gets a chance to see the animals close up, although in the case of the snakes and tarantula spiders you may not be too keen! However, as the Ranger talks about the animals and explains why even tarantulas are harmless unless challenged, everyone visibly relaxes and enjoys the 30 minute show.

The Critter Show was the highlight of the whole visit for me as it was so informative and well-presented. The Ranger handled a tarantula, a snapping turtle, a huge American turtle, an adorable white furry tamandua and a baby alligator. The Snake and Alligator Show is similarly informative and entertaining with a range of reptiles.

Additional Info

Throughout the year, Billie Swamp Safari hosts a number of special events. One of the most thrilling is the Big Cypress Shootout and Re-enactment of the Second Seminole War in late February. The 1830s re-enactment takes place in a grassy amphitheater and includes plenty of war-painted Indians on horseback ambushing soldiers. There is real cannon fire and soldiers can be seen loading and firing their flintlock muskets. The event includes alligator wrestling, Seminole Stomp Dancing and the opportunity for visitors to try their skills at tomahawk throwing and primitive archery. There is also a Soldier Camp and plenty of Native American craft stalls.

In June, Billie Swamp Safari hosts a Swamp Kids Summer Fun Festival and in mid-July there is a Folk Fest Nature Celebration with folk music, vendors and art works.

Tips
You definitely need to arrive early at the Billie Swamp Safari in order to enjoy the full range of attractions in the all-inclusive ticket price.

Wear a long sleeve shirt and hat to protect against the sun, and a liberal spraying of deet insect repellant as you are in the heart of the swamp.

Cost

Safari Day Package
Adults 13-61 $49.95
Seniors 62+ $45.95
Children 4-12 $35.95
Reduced admission (after 3.30pm) $30 all ages
Single Swamp Buggy or Airboat Tour
Adults 13-61 $25
Seniors/Children $25
Check out the website for discount coupons

Opening Times

Daily 9 a.m. to 6 p.m.

Where to Eat at Billie Swamp Safari

There are plenty of shady places for enjoying a picnic if you want to bring your own food. However, the Swamp Water Café is better than most attraction restaurants.

The well-priced menu is extensive with a good choice of burgers, hot sandwiches, catfish, huge salads and more unusual fare. It is well worth taking the opportunity to sample some of the foods not found elsewhere such as frog's legs, bison burgers and gator tail nuggets. There are sampler platters if you really cannot decide!

Nearby Attractions

- Ah-Tah-Thi-Ki Museum, showing the life and culture of the Florida Seminoles
- Clewiston
- Lake Okeechobee

Bird Gardens of Naples

In December 2011, Keriellen Lohrman and her husband Griffith bought five acres of land adjoining the Corkscrew Swamp Sanctuary and set about creating Keri's dream – a Rescue Center and Sanctuary for Exotic Birds. It is now a fully functioning haven for exotic birds and has become one of the top attractions in Naples.

The Bird Gardens are set in a natural Florida environment, surrounded by farmland and brimming with flowering plants, shady trees and countless colorful butterflies. It is now home to over 300 needy parrots, cockatoos, cockatiels and other beautiful exotic birds and is an absolute delight to visit.

Keri offers fascinating and informative private tours lasting up to two hours. Introducing each bird by name, she educates, inspires and regales visitors with tales of life with her feathered friends. Highlights are the chance to handfeed nuts to friendly Macaws and Nanday Conures in a walk-in aviary – the perfect opportunity to take some wonderful photographs as part of this superb tour.

Location
Located next to the Audubon Corkscrew Sanctuary just off Immokalee Road

Bird Gardens of Naples
1060 Purple Martin Drive
Naples
FL 34120
Tel: (813) 841-1911

https://birdgardensofnaples.org/

What to Expect on a Visit to Naples Bird Gardens
Tours begin near the car park beneath a shady arbor where Keriellen introduces herself and explains a little about the mission of the Bird Gardens Rescue Sanctuary. As parrots can live up to 80 years, they often outlive their owners and need a caring and understanding home, particularly if they have behavioral issues or are wild-caught and untamed.

The Bird Gardens of Naples offers a loving home to all such unfortunate or unwanted pets, as well as taking in birds that are too old for breeding or whose owners can no longer take care of them. Exotic birds are not allowed to be released into the wild, as they are considered an invasive species. Similarly, if wild native birds of prey are brought to the sanctuary for care, they have to be forwarded to a wildlife facility as the Bird Gardens are specifically for exotic birds.

During the introductory talk, you will hear the shrieks and calls from the parrots, macaws and other residents as they anticipate your visit. Paved trails run through an area of green ferns, palmettos, strawberry guavas, swamp poinsettia, milkweed, night-blooming cereus and shady native trees. Butterflies and insects abound in this federally protected natural area, so it's important to wear bug repellant for your visit.

Scattered along the trail are well-constructed aviaries, housing a variety of beautiful exotic birds either singly or in family groups. They have natural wood perches, breeding boxes and items to encourage foraging, such as pine cones. The constant care given to the birds through daily feeding, cleaning and raking their cages is very apparent, as all the cages are clean and well-maintained. The large Quarantine Room is filled with cages, some with birds available for adoption.

The first part of the tour has many beautiful cockatoos including one that lived in a call center and can mimic a phone ringing with eerie accuracy! Keri introduces Murphy and visitors can duck under the entrance and enter the aviary to handfeed him the nuts that are thoughtfully provided. It's a delightful experience as Murphy gently takes the nut from your hand and stores it in his mouth for enjoying later. He clearly knows the routine, for as we began to walk away he shrieked, scolded and cried! Further along we met Dennis and Nibbles – two critically endangered Lesser Sulfur-crested Cockatoos, of which only 1000 remain wild in their native Samoa.

Further along we saw Mango, a fabulous Umbrella Cockatoo, before reaching a cage of African Grey Parrots. They showed their intelligence by taking the nuts offered through the mesh, and promptly dropping them on the ground. They had already worked out that they got lots more nuts this way and could spend the rest of the day feasting on the dropped nuts once the stupid humans had moved on!

Next we saw Green Cheeked Conures and Quaker Parakeets (Monk Parakeets) and we listened to the story of how in 1971 a container of Quaker birds broke open in the port of New York City. These hardy birds now thrive in colonies from Chicago to the Keys!

The highlight of the tour was entering the large aviary of free-flying Red and Blue Macaws with their long colorful tails and vibrant plumage. There were about a dozen birds sitting expectantly on perches waiting to be fed nut treats, and we were all happy to oblige. Some boldly landed on outstretched arms while smaller green Nanday Conures (Black Hooded Parakeets) landed on heads and hats in search of a snack. It was a wonderful experience as everyone interacted with these beautiful rescue birds and got some amazing photographs.

We sampled ripe Surinam Cherries hanging over the path before reaching a larger flight housing many smaller cockatiels. They were part of a rescue when their owner died, leaving 125 free-flying untamed birds in his home. Apparently it took six days and many bites and scratches to secure the birds and re-house them in the Bird Gardens Sanctuary.

More aviaries held Yellow Collared Macaws, Amazon Parrots, Bolivian Military Macaws, Blue and Gold Macaws, pretty Indian Ringneck Parrots and more Scarlet Macaws that were separated due to behavioral issues. Many of the birds talked, shouting out "Hello," "Goodbye" or their favorite phrases to attract attention as we passed by.

One final highlight was seeing Big Bird perform by displaying his wings. He was part of the Key West Sunset Celebration Show for many years and is now enjoying his retirement entertaining visitors at the Bird Gardens of Naples.

Keri made a warm, knowledgeable and entertaining host who provides a wonderful tour to see some of nature's most vividly colored creatures in a Florida setting. The Bird Gardens of Naples provides a wonderful experience for all ages and fully deserves its place as one of Naples most popular attractions.

Additional Information

Although tours are free, the sanctuary is a nonprofit organization which relies on donations to feed, house and care for these amazing exotic birds. Donations of cash, equipment (see the website wish list), bird food and unsalted nuts (not peanuts) are always appreciated to help maintain this outstanding sanctuary.

You may wish to sponsor a bird by pledging a monthly amount starting at just $10, or adopt a bird that is in need of a good home.

Admission

Tours are free by prior arrangement; donations are welcome.

Opening Times

Tours are offered Thursday – Sunday at 11 a.m. and last up to 2 hours.

For security reasons, visitors must schedule a tour before visiting. Call the Bird Gardens (813-841-1911) or book your place on a tour via the website by submitting your name, email address and number of guests. It's easy!

Where to Eat near the Naples Bird Gardens

There are several pleasant waterfront restaurants in Bonita Springs. The award-winning Coconut Jacks on Bonita Beach Road serves food from 11 a.m. including fresh seafood, appetizers and key lime pie. Sit out on the deck overlooking the water and enjoy the atmosphere and wildlife.

Known for their ginormous subs packed with hand carved meat and fresh salad, Stan's Super Subs and Deli is a mouthwatering experience on Old 41 Road in Bonita Springs. It's more a hole-in-the-wall deli than a café but a great choice for food on the go.

Nearby Attractions
- Corkscrew Swamp Sanctuary
- Ave Maria
- Immokalee Pioneer Museum
- Lovers Key State Park
- Clam Pass Park

Clam Pass Beach and Boardwalk

Although the traffic on Tamiami Trail can make you feel that you are living in a busy city, places like Clam Pass Beach show the other side of Naples. Undeveloped green space, mangroves inhabited by native birds and wildlife and the chance to walk on the sand with the wind in your hair are hard to beat!

Clam Pass Beach is a little further south than the better-known Delnor-Wiggins Pass State Park. Access to the beach is along a boardwalk or via the electric tram shuttle if you're loaded down with beach chairs and equipment. Once you hit the beach you can enjoy swimming, wildlife spotting and floating in the natural lazy river as you ride the tide.

Location

Located 6 miles north of central Naples at Seagate Drive/Clayton Rd near the Naples Grande Resort Hotel

Clam Pass Beach
410 Seagate Drive
Naples
FL 34103
Tel: (239) 254-4000

https://www.colliergov.net/index.aspx?page=458

What to Expect on a Visit to Clam Pass Beach and Boardwalk

The 35-acre site at Clam Pass Beach manages to offer far more than other beaches in the area. You can enjoy:

- Guided nature walks
- Train ride to and from the beach
- Boardwalk through the mangroves
- Birds and wildlife
- Dolphins and turtles
- Shelling
- Sandy beach
- Swimming and tubing on the tidal flow
- Watersports and equipment rentals
- Concessions and snacks

You need to arrive early on weekends to secure one of the public parking spaces. From there a broad boardwalk, made entirely out of recycled milk cartons, runs for almost ¾ mile through the shrubby mangroves and around the saltwater lagoon of Outer Clam Bay to reach the beach. It's a peaceful walk but it obviously deters some beachgoers, so the beach is rarely crowded.

Once on the white sandy beach you can enjoy swimming in the clear turquoise waters of the Gulf or go sailing or kayaking from the beach. There is a watersports concession offering rentals of aqua bikes, kayaks, watersports equipment, beach chairs and umbrellas to save carrying everything from the parking lot. Bring a cooler of drinks and a picnic or make use of the beach restaurant and bar for refreshments, ice cream and drinks. There are also restrooms on the beach.

The boardwalk runs through three kinds of protected mangrove trees: red, black and white. Red mangroves are the tallest with a reddish color wood and blunt-ended leaves. Black mangroves have smaller elliptical leaves with a hairy underside and white mangroves are the smallest bushes with oval leaves that are rounded at both ends.

If I sound incredibly knowledgeable, that's because I have joined in one of the excellent nature walks provided by volunteers of the Conservancy of Southwest Florida. Just turn up at the tram stop at 9 a.m. Monday to Saturday in the winter season (December to April) and join the free tour. Who knows what you will see and learn about!

Wildlife at Clam Pass Beach is diverse and plentiful. The mangroves provide shelter for fish and invertebrates and wading birds are always on the lookout for some tasty food. Sea turtles come ashore to lay their eggs on the beach in the summer months. If you walk along the water's edge looking for shells you may see dolphins just offshore along with gliding pelicans.

The most fun is riding gently in the natural lazy river that runs in and out of Clam Pass with the tide. The water is rarely too deep to stand up so it is a safe ride for swimmers. Just bring your tube or inflatable toy and enjoy the experience.

Admission

There is a parking fee of $8 for those who do not have a Beach Parking Permit.

Guided nature walks and the train ride are currently free of charge.

Opening Times

The beach is open daily from 8 a.m. to sundown.

Where to Eat at Clam Pass Beach

The beachside restaurant/ snack bar is run by a local hotel and has excellent menu choices and high standards. Concession stands sell drinks and snacks, or bring your own picnic.

Nearby Attractions

- Delnor-Wiggins Pass State Park
- Bird Gardens of Naples
- Koreshan State Historic Site

Collier County Museum

Collier County is the third largest county in Florida in area, and is even larger than the state of Delaware. Discover the history of this beautiful county, which can be traced for thousands of years. The biggest changes have taken place over the last 100 years and these developments are all recorded in the Collier County Museum, which gives a fascinating insight into this desirable county that attracts millions of visitors and winter residents every year.

This award-winning flagship museum has excellent indoor galleries and exhibits as well as 17 other monuments, buildings, vehicles and features in the five-acre outdoor park. See some of the everyday tools, ceremonial masks and items the Calusa Indian left behind which were unearthed by local archaeologists, then step outside and visit a recreated Shell Mound and Seminole Village.

More recent settler history is also celebrated in the museum exhibits, with information, displays, human interest stories and artifacts about cracker homes, fishing, railroads, trail building, hurricanes and even oil drilling in the county.

Suitable for all ages, this free museum is a wonderful place to introduce youngsters to local history with visual displays and exhibits ranging from a replica Seminole War Fort to a typical 1926 Naples Cottage.

Location
Located on Tamiami Trail E (Us 41/90) southeast of downtown Naples in the Collier County Government Complex

Collier County Museum
Collier County Government Complex
3331 Tamiami Trail E
Naples
FL34112
Tel: (239) 252-8476

www.colliermuseums.com/locations/collier_museum

What to Expect on a Visit to Collier County Museum
The museum is located on Hwy-41/90 at the rear of the Collier County Government Complex. There is dedicated free parking for museum patrons outside the museum

building. Enter the welcome area and a volunteer docent will greet you with an informative Visitor Guide, map and information about the museum and its exhibits.

Follow the glass fronted displays and storyboards around the 10,000 square-foot main gallery and exhibition hall which is laid out in chronological order. Displays include the early Megalodons and archaeological finds in the area including skulls, shells and Spanish *reales* (silver coins). Primitive weights, pottery shards and huge handmade nails date back to the early 16th century when the Spanish Empire captured and colonized Florida.

From the colorful Conquistador era, Collier County history moves forward to the 1700s when the Seminoles and Creek Indians arrived to escape the white settlement further north. Exhibits show their colorful dress and extraordinary lives these hardy Indians carved out in the swamps, fishing and trading. After the Third Seminole War, pioneers were attracted to Florida by the Land Settlement Act. This is reflected in dioramas of early settler homes and dress.

Learn about the crackers, rum runners, railroad builders, plume hunters, clam diggers, hermits and cattle drovers that made their living in this inhospitable wilderness. Follow the story of the trail builders and those who worked as loggers in Big Cypress, described as "the toughest job in the US, and possibly the world." Wood was exported out by trains – another important part of 20th century development in Southwest Florida. After learning about Humble Oil at Sunniland Oil Field, World War 2 training in Naples, Hurricane Donna and Gary Cooper films shot in Naples, the museum continues outside.

Outdoor Exhibits

The shady park has winding paved paths connecting the many relocated buildings and exhibits shown on your map. First stop is the Logging Locomotive, built in 1910 by the Baldwin Locomotive Works in Pennsylvania and known as "The Deuce."

Explore the Orchid House with is tumbling stream as you head for the Huntoon Gallery where you can peek through the windows at the taxidermy collection of Dr Earl L. Baum in this 1938 home.

Check out the Kokomis Ferry which took passengers to the private Keewaydin Club on the largest unbridged island of the 10,000 islands. This basic ferry was used from 1934 to 1999 to carry supplies and visitors across Gordon Pass to Keewaydin Island.

The primitive Swamp Buggy is worth viewing. It was built from salvaged parts by Ed Frank, Naples first mechanic and garage owner. The sturdy truck chassis and extraordinary wheels made it ideal for hauling cypress or hunting in the swampy land that still engulfed Collier County in the 1920s.

The Craighead Laboratory is the restored working lab of Everglades' scientist Dr Frank C. Craighead Sr. (1889-1982). He studied native Florida plants and a recreated Native Garden of endemic tree and plant species is a memorial to this Naples pioneer. The boardwalk continues around to the gazebo, passing benches, ferns, palms and quiet shady areas of this peaceful city park.

One of the largest buildings on the museum site is the two-story Naples Cottage, furnished and equipped as it would have been for owner William Peters in 1926. Rescued from demolition, the cottage was transported to the museum site and can now be explored as part of your visit.

Pass the traditional Chickee, an open-sided Indian hut with a thatched roof of Sabal Palm leaves, and see the sugar press with its dual rollers that would have been animal powered in 1914, when it was in use. A wooden Trading Post building can be seen just before the Calusa Indian Mound which was built of discarded shells and trash. Decorated with huge whelk shells, some mounds were used as burial mounds and other were used for creating a raised island for building a chickee above any storm surge. There are various chickee structures in this recreated Seminole Camp showing the sleeping platform and rafters where items would have been stored.

Finish the tour with a walk around the Palisade Fort and a look at the 1940 M4 Sherman Tank.

The tour ends in the Exhibition/Lecture Hall before returning through the Visitor Center which has a small gift shop with a good range of local books.

Admission
Free

Opening Times
Open Monday to Saturday 9 a.m. to 4 p.m. Closed national and county holidays.

Where to Eat near the Collier County Museum
The museum park provides picnic tables for those wanting to bring a picnic.

Nearby Attractions
- Naples Zoo
- Tin City
- Corkscrew Swamp Sanctuary

Corkscrew Swamp Sanctuary

Located in the Western Everglades, Corkscrew Swamp Sanctuary and the Blair Audubon Center provide an amazing and informative experience of native Florida wildlife.

The 13,000 acre wildlife preserve takes its name from the Corkscrew River (now known as the Imperial River) which meanders with deep twists and turns through the region. The National Audubon Society has protected the area as a bird sanctuary since 1912 and it is home to over 200 species of birds.

During the 1940s and 50s when native cypress trees were being felled at an alarming rate, it became apparent that this area needed to be further protected as a conservation area and wildlife habitat. In 1954, 14 separate organizations joined with the National Audubon Society and the first area of swamp and cypress was purchased. At that time the area was almost inaccessible, so a boardwalk was built enabling visitors to enjoy the birds and wildlife without having any impact on the environment.

Location
20 miles east of Bonita Springs off CR 846.

375 Sanctuary Road West
Naples
FL34120
Tel: (239) 348-9151

www.corkscrew.audubon.org/

What to Expect at Corkscrew Swamp Sanctuary

Visitors will find that the Corkscrew Swamp Sanctuary covers six distinct areas of different habitat: Bald Cypress, Pond Cypress, Wet Prairie, Sawgrass Pond, Pine Flatwood, and Central Marsh, all easily viewed from the shady 2.25 mile long boardwalk.

First stop is at the Blair Audubon Center where information, a nature store, café and exhibits can be seen.

Purchase your admission ticket here before heading into the theater for a 14-minute informative sound and light presentation. Visitors stand in the theater and listen to the bird calls, the growl of an alligator and the strange barks of tree frogs as the presentation highlights the various residents of this reserve. You can hire binoculars for $3 or pick up a free stroller or wheelchair to enhance your visit.

The boardwalk is made of sustainable pau-lope hardwood which blends into the natural scenery as it is covered in patches of lichen. Although the full length of the boardwalk circuit is over 2 miles, there is a shortcut to return along a shorter loop if required.

It is fascinating to stroll along within touching distance of ancient bald cypress, palms, ferns, flowering shrubs, and marsh plants. If you stop to look carefully, the marsh plants are covered in tiny white, yellow, red and blue flowers which can easily be missed, so do take your time!

With the help of the Companion Field Guide to the reserve ($2) we identified pickerelweed, broad leaved arrowheads, buttonbush, water dropwort, and even the solitary red bloom of an enormous swamp hibiscus. Air plants (epiphytes) were perched in tree crevices and in one area strangler figs could be seen creating a sturdy support network on their chosen host tree.

Bird song, insect noises, twitters and shrieks add natural background noise. The sound carries over the still wetland, so do be aware that your voice can be heard far away too!

We heard a woodpecker hammering into the top of a huge cypress tree and the squawks and grunts of vultures squabbling over a tasty kill. Bright orange Ruddy Daggerwing Butterflies flit around, clearly in butterfly paradise, and we saw hairy caterpillars, wading birds and many spiders on their perfectly formed webs.

If I sound incredibly knowledgeable, then I'll let you into a secret. The boardwalk is patrolled by rangers who are happy to stop, answer questions, and identify flowers and creatures. They also walk the boardwalk adding temporary signs to the balustrades pointing out the web of a spotted orb weaver, or a black and yellow argiope spider with its long black and yellow banded legs. These useful signs helped us to spot nesting sites, a yellow rat snake sleeping in the hole of a tree and a rare ghost orchid high in a tree. There are also a series of interpretive boards giving bite-sized chunks of information as you walk.

One ranger had a selection of exhibits that drew quite a crowd. Children held the young alligator, saw a hollow alligator tooth, and learned about why the alligator has bumps on its back.

The gentle amble around with detours to viewpoints and the Marsh Observation Platform takes 1-2 hours, depending on how many plants and creatures you want to stop and photograph, but it is a wonderfully pleasant walk. I have never seen such variety of plants and trees which were enhanced by the information available. Even if you visit on a sunny day (I visited in October when it was still 90°F), there is plenty of shade and a gentle breeze at times.

Finish your visit and support this wonderful charity further by having a drink or snack in the café and browsing the excellent range of books and gifts in the nature store.

Additional Info

You may want to return to Corkscrew Swamp Sanctuary and join one of their monthly Corkscrew After Hours evening projects which have a theme of bats, bird migration, stargazing and other topics. Specialists are brought in to enhance the educational experience, with equipment such as telescopes and a bat detector to listen as the bats forage and feed. Hear hooting owls, croaking frogs, identify planets and stars, and spot the glowing amber eyes of alligators under a bright moon.

The After Hours Project offers a walk in this ancient forest with a totally different perspective from a daytime visit. There is no additional cost beyond the regular admission price. Simply turn up between 6.45 and 9pm on selected dates and learn something new!

Admission Cost (valid for 2 consecutive days)
Adults $12
Students (3-18) $6

Opening Times
Daily 7 a.m. to 5.30 p.m.
Monthly Corkscrew After Hours Event until 9 p.m.

Where to Eat at Corkscrew Swamp Sanctuary
The onsite tearoom has indoor and outdoor seating for visitors to enjoy refreshments. It offers fresh sandwiches and salads supplied daily by Taste Buds Custom Catering.

If you prefer to bring your own picnic, there are picnic tables in the car park area.

A long-term Naples favorite restaurant on Tamiami Trail in North Naples is the Pewter Mug restaurant. Famous for its "Almost World Famous Prime Rib" and all-you-can-eat soup and salad bar, this is an excellent venue to end a pleasant day out. Sous Chef Mike Pilarski has been ageing and hand cutting the Certified Angus Beef for over 40 years. The Lounge Bar of this local landmark opens at 4.30 p.m. and dining is from 5 p.m. to 9 p.m. daily.

Nearby Attractions
- Naples Zoo
- Naples Bird Gardens
- Koreshan State Historic Site

Koreshan State Historic Site

The Koreshan State Historic Site is a very unique and interesting place to visit. It is the preserved site of a 19th century religious community with 11 original buildings, Victorian gardens, a nature trail along the Estero River, canoeing and camp sites in a 200-acre park.

Self-guided tour leaflets and information boards are available, along with volunteer docents, for those who want to tour the grounds at their own pace. However, I can recommend taking a 90-minute ranger-led tour for those wanting to delve into the beliefs of Dr. Cyrus Teed and understand the day-to-day operations of his "New Jerusalem".

Koreshanity began in Estero in 1893 and lasted until 1982 when the last member died. Along with tours, the historic estate hosts the Estero Concert Series which attracts professional musicians and world class opera singers to perform in the atmospheric Art Hall. It also offers re-enactments and ghost walks at Halloween which are well worth attending.

Location
Koreshan is located at the intersection of US 41 and Corkscrew Road at Estero.

Koreshan State Historic Site
3800 Corkscrew Road
Estero
FL33928
Tel: (239) 992-0311

www.floridastateparks.org/koreshan/

What to Expect on a Historic Walking Tour
At the entrance, pay the admission and book a place on the next guided tour if you want a ranger-led experience of the historic site and gardens. The tour meets just off the car park outside the Art Hall, where a huge swamp mahogany provides shade from the Florida sun.

The tour begins in the beautiful Art Hall which is still used for public concerts as in the days of the Koreshan Unity Settlement. The hall is filled with artworks by former Koreshan members and by Dr. Teed's son, Douglas Arthur Teed, who became a well-known landscape and portrait artist in New York. The most remarkable exhibit is the globe which shows the world as we know it, but on the inner shell of the earth's outer atmosphere, as Dr. Teed believed it was.

We followed our knowledgeable volunteer guide, Mila, along the crushed shell paths passing Orchid Trees in full bloom, a Sabal Palm with cacti growing on the trunk and finally reached the cherry orchard just outside the Planetary Court building.

Here we learned more about Dr. Teed and his "illumination" in 1869 which led him to Chicago and then to Estero to found his Koreshan Unity, the word "Koreshan" being Persian for "shepherd". His new order followed a mix of Old Testament, Far Eastern ideas, reincarnation and Teed's own scientific beliefs. His ultimate aim was to define the universe through science.

About 3,000 members lived outside the settlement with their families while up to 300 others chose to join the religious order at Koreshan, which required giving their property to the community and living celibate lives onsite. The followers were hard-working people and the community was self-sufficient, even providing services to the outside community. They valued education and the arts and had their own drama group and 17-piece orchestra which performed public concerts.

The three-story Planetary Court is a fine example of Georgia Foursquare architecture, built in 1904. The cream clapboard house with its shady front porch was home to the Seven "Sisters" who provided much of the original finance Teed required to establish his community and saw to the day-to-day business of the settlement. Each lady had her own simply furnished room and a caretaker looked after them and lived at the top of the house in the cupola. We admired the ornate craftsman-built staircase made of beautiful date pine, and learned that there were no baths or kitchen in the house as the Sisters ate formally each evening at the communal dining area.

All the buildings are on the National Register of Historic Places, but there was never a church on site. We peeped inside the bakery which once made up to 600 loaves a day – the yeast bread was in great demand locally as it was so much tastier than the local cornbread. Other buildings include the two-room Vesta Newcombe building, final home to Vesta who arrived at the community as a child and lived here until her death in her 90s. We also saw the industrial area with a huge oil-driven generator which powered band saws and machinery in the neighboring machine shops as well as providing power to the surrounding outlying farms.

The Koreshan Unity was totally dependent upon Dr. Teed and after his death in 1908 many followers became disillusioned when his teachings about his resurrection were not fulfilled. Eventually the Koreshan community, its archives and substantial acreage were donated to the state of Florida in 1961.

The final part of the tour took us through the gardens where there are many specimen trees sourced by Dr. Teed on his travels all over the world. Look for the huge Australian Monkey Puzzle Tree, the exotic flowers on the Bombax (red silk cotton tree), the Ear Tree and the African Sausage Tree. Fruit trees, pecans, magnolias and lovely red pineapples with their exotic pink fruits can be enjoyed as well as more common azaleas and palms.

Landscaped mounds make a popular place for the burrowing Gopher Tortoises and two decorative bridges were an interesting highlight. Massive Washingtonian Palms planted in 1896 line the Grande Promenade which is visible from the Bamboo Landing. Here we saw many canoeists paddling in the clear shallow waters of the Estero

River, which was the main access to the settlement before US41 was paved. This area is the start of the Nature Trail, a pleasant 30-minute walk along the river ending at the boat ramp. I recommend going out and back along the river trail which is much more pleasant than returning on the park roads. Otters, herons, bobcats, foxes, alligators, snakes and a variety of birds of prey all make their home in the park.

Our tour ended at the Founders House, built for Cyrus Teed in 1896 and surprisingly comfortably furnished. There is an interesting display of old photographs of the Koreshan community in its heyday and an informative PBS film gives more background detail to this religious sect.

Additional Info

There is an excellent Guide to the Koreshan Unity Settlement with a brief history, map and details of each building. The Self-guided Tour of the Gardens brochure is filled with information and has a numbered plan of the main specimen plants and trees. Both these brochures are available from a display box as you walk along the concrete footpath from the car park to the Art Hall. Suggested donations of 50c per brochure are requested.

Cost

Park Admission

$2 for walkers and cyclists
$4 per vehicle and up to 8 passengers

Guided Walking Tour

$2 per adult; $1 for under 12s

Canoe hire

$5 per hour; $25 for the day
Canoe Rentals are handled at the Entrance Ranger Station

Opening Times

The park is open 8 a.m. to sundown daily

Guided Walking Tours of the Historic Site

January-March guided tours take place daily at 10 a.m. and 2 p.m.

April-December at 10 a.m. Saturdays and Sundays only

Guided tours can also be scheduled in advance on request.

Where to Eat near Koreshan State Historic Site

Estero has a number of family-run restaurants which finish off your visit to Koreshan perfectly.

Cocina Mexicana El Tenampa is a husband and wife Mexican restaurant on South Tamiami Trail (US 41) which is renowned for its quesadillas and delicious Texas burritos.

 Just down the road from Koreshan is the award-winning Tony Sacco's Coal Oven Pizza on Plaza del Lago Drive or try Hemingway's Island Grill for great handcrafted "island" food at the same location.

Nearby Attractions
- Naples Zoo
- Clam Pass Beach
- Corkscrew Swamp Sanctuary

Museum of the Everglades

Don't be misled by the name of this lovely attraction in the heart of historic Everglades City. It is not a museum about the wildlife of the Everglades, but rather a museum about the history of Everglades City and the building of the Tamiami Trail. This informative, well-laid out museum is well worth spending a short time visiting, and admission is free.

Location

Located 4 miles south of Tamiami Trail in the heart of historic Everglades City.

Museum of the Everglades
105 West Broadway
Everglades City
FL34139
(239) 695-0008

www.evergladesmuseum.org

What to Expect on a Visit to the Museum of the Everglades

The historic building which now accommodates the Museum of the Everglades was originally built by Barron Collier as a community laundry in 1927. It was part of the planned community of Everglades City which he founded in 1923. The laundry served the city well until 1942, when lack of staff and laundry forced the business to close.

The building was used as an insurance office, barber shop, place of worship and pizzeria before becoming the administrative center of the Collier County Development Corporation. In 1965 the old laundry became the meeting hall of the Everglades Women's Club. They eventually purchased the building in 1972 and donated it to the County in 1988 to be used as a museum. The building was restored by the Friends of the Museum of the Everglades in conjunction with the city, state and county government. The Museum of the Everglades opened to the public in 1998, significantly on the 70th anniversary of the opening of the Tamiami Trail. This charming building is now listed on the National Register of Historic Places.

The museum curator will give you a personal welcome before you start your self-guided tour of the exhibits, photographs, models and displays in the open museum hall. It is well laid out with information about the first settlers in the area, the Seminole and Miccosukee people. See the dried gator hide and read about the illegal trade of bird feathers, gator hide and moonshine in this area, particularly during Prohibition.

Other museum displays cover local businesses such as the Bank of the Everglades (1923-1962), tomato growing, grapefruit canning, old school history and the naval base and coast guard patrols that were based in the area during World War 2. In 1943 the oil and timber resources were discovered in the Everglades and the extensive logging of huge cypress trees became known as "probably the most difficult job in the USA."

The storyboards and photographs showing the building of the Tamiami Trail are fascinating. The route received its name as it connected Tampa with Miami, although it became known as Florida's Appian Way.

Everglades City was the base for the Tamiami Trail Project which started in 1916 but was not completed until 1928. Workers struggled with almost unsurmountable physical problems as they toiled in the heat, dealing with snakes, mosquitos, alligators, solid rock and drainage on a massive scale. Even the Floating Steam Dredge sunk on arrival! It was acknowledged that the Tamiami Trail would never have been completed without the financial support of Barron Collier, after whom the new County was named.

Final exhibits in the museum include an account of the city's destruction by Hurricane Donna's 160mph winds in 1960. This led to the county seat being moved to Naples, which was less isolated and by then had a well-developed infrastructure.

Additional Information

Just 4 miles east of Hwy 29 on the Tamiami Trail (US-41) is the Big Cypress Swamp National Preserve Welcome Center. There are always huge gators lying on the banks of the slough which can easily be seen from the boardwalk. The Welcome Center has some excellent exhibits and information about the wildlife on the Everglades and has an interesting film about the swamp and its resources.

Admission

Free

Opening Times

Open Monday-Saturday 9 a.m. to 4 p.m.

Where to Eat in Everglades City

There are plenty of places to eat in Everglades City, but choose a restaurant on the waterfront for great views of birds, fish and buzzing with activity from departing airboats.

The Magnolia Street Grill is a popular restaurant which has a vintage yellow VW Beetle parked outside. The open-air deck, terrace and gardens are decorated with strings of old fishing floats, pergolas and shady seating areas. It offers excellent views across the basin on the Barron River to the lighthouse. Service is friendly and the menu is typical American burgers, shrimp and fried fish.

Neighboring City Seafood is an open air wooden shack sitting on the water. Order at the bar from an extensive menu of sandwiches, burgers and baskets of fried seafood, then take your seat at one of the bench tables and enjoy the atmosphere and view. The complex also has an ice cream counter with a choice of flavors of hand scooped ice cream for a refreshing dessert.

Nearby Attractions
- Naples Zoo
- Naples Botanical Gardens
- Florida Panther National Wildlife Refuge (Trails)

Naples Botanical Garden

Known as the "Gardens with Latitude", Naples Botanical Garden focuses on plants found between the 26th latitude south and the 26th latitude north, where Naples Florida is located. The gardens are a colorful showcase of exotic blooms and they succeed in their aim to conserve, engage and inspire visitors of all ages.

The nine themed gardens include a Brazilian Garden, Caribbean Garden, Asian Garden, Florida Garden, Water Garden and Children's Garden including a Butterfly Garden. The 170-acre site also provides a magnificent setting for the annual Naples Flower show, temporary art exhibitions, concerts and special events.

The three-dimensional landscaping has a succession of landscaped gardens, water features and preserves on various different levels so you frequently find yourself looking up or down at different views. The higher elevations are refreshingly breezy as you explore the meandering paths along the Uplands Trail or around Deep Lake to the birding tower.

Location
Just 10 minutes from downtown Naples, south of US41 on the corner of Bayshore and Thomasson Drive.

4820 Bayshore Drive
Naples
FL34112

Tel: 239.643.7275 / 877.433.1874

www.naplesgarden.org

What to Expect at the Naples Botanical Garden
First impressions are positive as you walk from the parking lot towards the entrance to the gardens. There are some wonderful flowering shrubs along the walkways, whetting the appetite for more colorful surprises inside the garden – and you will not be disappointed!

After paying the admission fee and getting your map to the garden, explore some of the exotic tropical landscaping lining the boardwalk. The lush foliage surrounding the shady pool in Kathryn's Garden is followed by a collection of wonderful plants of charisma in Irma's Garden.

The spiny parrot palm and giant bottle tree show nature at its most diverse. In contrast, the paved courtyard and of the Orchid Garden provide a tranquil setting for over 1,000 species of naturalized orchids around an established tabebuia tree. Located between the well-stocked Garden Shop, Kapnick Hall and the Fogg Café, it is popular starting point for most visitors.

The gardens are colorful in all seasons from spring flowering blooms on the Silk Floss trees through stunning fall color. In early summer, the red flowering poncianas burst into bloom along with purple jacarandas and fragrant plumerias (frangipani).

The first departure from the main path is into the Children's Garden. This is far larger and more complex than you might expect, with a fountain splash area, miniature Cracker-style house and garden providing a plethora of interactive experiences for young visitors. Stepping stones, a crawl net and a wooden observation tower with a suspended bridge make exploring fun.

Within the garden is the mesh butterfly house, well planted with the favorite blooms of butterflies and a helpful chart for identifying the fluttering residents. Vibrant mosaic benches and planters brighten the area as you stroll towards the pergola with its swing bench seats. And there's more! A concrete path with pressed leaves leads to a sand play area.

Back on the main footpath, the tiered waterfall cascade draws the eye across a lake of purple flowering lotus and water lilies. Ducks, frogs, herons and dragonflies are all in evidence here. This signals the start of the Brazilian Garden, which perfectly captures the vivid colors and joie de vivre of that hot and vibrant country. Huge bromeliads line the winding footpath as you walk beside the lake. Red stemmed porteas with their bright purple flowers are one of my favorites, along with the dangling scarlet and yellow flowers of lobster claw heliconias.

All the plants are clearly labeled for the curious, and additional information boards tell of a plant's use for dye, food coloring or cosmetics. Once you reach the top of the waterfall, a surprise awaits! An infinity-edge lily pond is the source of the waterfall and it gives a stunning foreground to views across the gardens. Giant Amazon waterlilies with their broad rimmed leaves are scattered across the still water. Their fragrant white blooms open in the evening and then close at dusk, trapping Scarab beetles overnight. These pollinators do a good job of covering themselves in pollen before their release the following day. After enjoying the panoramic view, descend to the pier and see the waterfall from a different angle.

The Asian Garden is full of tropical color around the Balinese shrine where you can sit in the shade and sip chilled water which is thoughtfully provided here. Close by is the Thai Pavilion with its distinctive vented roof and Balinese wooden benches. The Javanese ruins and temple structures define the area well and give a structured backdrop to the exotic flowers. Rivers and bridges add to the pleasure of the garden with the sound of running water. Tall stands of yellow-stemmed bamboo rustle in the breeze and there is even a small paddy field growing long grain rice.

The Caribbean Gardens are depicted by the white and turquoise Chattel House building with its Geiger trees and banana plants nearby. Look out for the arbor covered in purple flowers of the Queen's Wreath (Petrea volubilis) which flowers several times a year. The Ideas Garden is next to the Wildflower Meadow and Florida Garden, with its bougainvillea and Palm Circle where mockingbirds clearly recognize the palmettos as home territory! One final area to enjoy is the Enabling Garden with raised beds and vertical planters.

Finish back in the Visitor Center where the well-stocked Gift Shop has an excellent selection of plants, books and gifts for garden lovers.

Additional Info about Naples Botanical Garden

Naples Botanical Garden was developed comparatively recently, in 2009, on 170 acres. The opportunity to design a garden from scratch provided a blank canvas which was used to its full potential, creating undulating paths through a series of themed gardens showcasing plants and cultures from around the world. During the original planning, land was set aside for the uplands and wetlands preserves to conserve rare and endangered plants and a population of gopher tortoises. Designed by a team of some of the world's leading landscape designers, the garden has since been extended to include a 25,000 square-foot Visitor Center, retail space and the delightful Fogg Café around the entrance.

An important part of the garden's survival is the team of 700 volunteers who help out with many essential tasks. The 6,500 family members provide ongoing support for the gardens while benefitting from unlimited free access and special members-only events.

Water is a common feature linking one garden with the next and the gardens received an award for Intelligent Use of Water. The Executive Director received the Award of Merit from the American Gardens Association and they were Florida's School Garden of the Year. More recently they were voted "The Best Place to Take Grandparents" by Gulfshore Life!

Cost
Adults $14.95
Children aged 4-14 $9.95

Opening Times
9 a.m. to 5 p.m. daily; Tuesdays 8 a.m. to 5 p.m.

Where to Eat Around the Naples Botanical Garden

It's a good idea to plan your visit over lunchtime so you can enjoy the delightful indoor/outdoor setting and inventive menu at Fogg Café. The restaurant menu offers creative dishes using sustainable seasonal produce, including some tropical fruits and vegetables grown in the garden.

The menu follows the international theme of the gardens with Caribbean, Asian, Brazilian and Floridian influences. Enjoy healthy vegetable wraps, tasty salads, soups and burgers. Sweet treats include frozen yoghurt and delicious warm banana bread with butter and local honey to accompany your cappuccino or pot of tea. The premises are licensed and have a good choice of wine and chilled European beer.

No outside food and drink is permitted in the gardens.

Tips

Visit from November to April and join one of the guided tours which take place daily at 11 a.m.

Dog walks are offered at certain times on Sundays, Tuesdays and Thursdays – check the website for times. There is a fee for non-member dogs.

Nearby Attractions
- Collier County Museum
- Tin City
- Naples Zoo

Naples Depot Museum

Housed in the historic depot of the Naples Seaboard Air Line Railway Station, the Naples Depot Museum is a fascinating collection of exhibits, photographs, and archives of Naples history from a transportation viewpoint. It shows how early settlers used technology and transportation to develop this swampy final frontier.

As well as featuring the old railway station and several restored railcars, the museum covers the Calusa Indians and their dugout canoes, boat building history, the early mule-pulled Naples taxi wagon, fishing boats, the original Frank Tumble Bug Swamp Buggy, and the role of Naples airport during World War 2. Throw in a few local characters and a couple of hurricanes and you have a very pleasant place to pass away an hour or two in a building now listed on the National Register of Historic Places.

Location
Located north/east of the Tamiami Trail on the corner of 5th Ave and 10th Street.

Naples Depot Museum
1051 5th Avenue South
Naples
FL34102
Tel: (239) 262-6526

www.colliermuseums.com/locations/naples_depot

What to Expect at the Naples Depot Museum
Naples was only put on the map when the railroad arrived, allowing developers, and subsequently winter visitors, to reach this desirable Gulf Coast location. As the museum exhibits show, Naples was actually reached by two rival railroads within 10 days of each other in 1927. The Naples Miami Railroad arrived just ahead of the Seaboard Air Line Railway's inaugural Orange Blossom Special complete with Pullman cars. Trains ran from the depot from 1927 to 1971, opening up Southwest Florida to tourism.

Explore the displays of railroad china and silverware in the former Black Passenger Waiting Room. The room has excellent interpretive displays, maps and old photos. Linger a while and you will witness the sights and sounds of a steam train arriving just outside the window! It's a wonderful audio-visual effect.

The museum focuses on local Naples characters such as Orlo "Kit" Carson, the last stationmaster to serve at the Naples Depot.

Other galleries include Calusa and Seminole history with a primitive dugout canoe on display along with shells, arrowheads and fossilized bones dating back over 8,000 years. The Calusa hand-dug the Old Naples Canal which was six feet deep and 30 feet wide in places.

Further displays include the mule-pulled wagon which was used by William Pulling and his family from 1915 to drive along the sand and oyster shell streets of Naples.

Walk up the incline to the exhibit of Naples in the Automobile Age and get acquainted with Naples pioneers such as Speed Menefee, Naples' fifteen-minute Mayor, the Prince family, Omah A. Clarke, Mamie Tooke and many more influential figures who settled in Naples in the early 20th century. Displays on Prohibition (Naples on the Gulp), Keewaydin Island, fishing, boat building and Naples in Flight give a fascinating insight into the not-so-distant past as the city of Naples developed.

One amazing piece of history is the Tumble Bug Swamp Buggy, built by Ed and William Frank who ran the local garage and service station. Originally used for hunting and Swamp Buggy Racing, the vehicle was present in local parades as recently as 1951.

Important events in Naples' past are shown, including the building of Port Royal, the legacy of Hurricane Donna in 1960 and the building of Alligator Alley (now the I-75) from 1964-68.

The final gallery is used for a range of temporary exhibits. A door leads outside to the restored railcars which are walk-through exhibits. The silver Seaboard Observation Lounge Car #6601 was built by the Budd Company in 1947. It is complete with shocking pink, scarlet and red leather bench seats around tables with a bar at one end of the railcar.

The more basic Railroad Caboose has wooden seats, a desk and storage and acted as the office for the conductor. Steps lead up to the cupola which was used by the conductor for 360 degree views. This traditional conductor's car was in use for 140 years until the 1980s when two-way radios finally rendered them obsolete.

Additional Information

Located in the grounds of the Naples Depot Museum is the Naples Lionel Train Museum with multi-level train displays, including Thomas the Tank Engine, to delight all railway enthusiasts.

Checkout the website for full information www.naplestrainmuseum.org

Admission to Naples Depot Museum

Free

Opening Times

Monday – Saturday 9 a.m. to 4 p.m. Closed on national and county holidays.

Where to Eat near the Naples Depot Museum

Newly opened on Tamiami Trail near Trader Joes, Red Robin Gourmet Burgers offers over two dozen different gourmet burgers to satisfy all tastes. The bottomless Steak Fries mean you get a continuous supply of hot tasty fries whether you choose salads, sandwiches, burgers or the crispiest battered Arctic cod served with a side of tartare sauce – my personal favorite treat!

Closer to the museum, Tin City has a choice of waterfront restaurants and cafés in an authentic Old Naples setting.

Nearby Attractions

- Naples Zoo
- Corkscrew Swamp
- Tin City

Naples Segway Tours

Naples Segway Tours are a great way to combine an informative tour of Naples' history and highlights with a novel activity. You soon get the hang of riding/driving the Segway and it covers a lot more ground than a walking tour. This trip is particularly fun for teenagers (14+) and those interested in experiencing a Segway for themselves.

Copyright Gillian Birch

Location
Located in the heart of downtown Naples
Naples Segway Tours
1010 6th Ave
Naples
Florida FL 34102
Tel: (239) 262-7205 or 1-800-592-0848

http://www.segwayofnaples.com/

What to Expect on a Naples Segway Tour

Segway tours are conducted in small groups and they all start with a short safety video. After donning a helmet and earpiece, everyone gets a personal training session to master the Segway.

These gravity-defying machines are certainly a fun way to get around. Just lean forward to move forward and accelerate and lean slightly backwards to stop or reverse (yes they do go backwards!). Use the twist grip handles to turn left and right. You can see why Segways are fun for all ages, although you have to be at least 14 years of age to join the Naples tour.

Once everyone has shown themselves to be proficient, the tour sets off behind the guide to discover some of Naples most interesting and historic sites. You need to keep up to remain in radio contact with the guide through the radio headset. Regular stops for short talks along the way give you an insight into the history and development of Naples over the last 120 years.

The tour takes in the old seaport and docks, Landing Park and the boats and art galleries at Crayton Cove before zipping along 12th Ave South to Palm Cottage, the oldest surviving home in the city.

Moving on from there you will head for historic Naples Pier, one of the earliest structures in the city, before riding between the beautiful homes on 3rd Street South to Roger Park. There's a stop outside St Ann's church before experiencing the upscale shops and restaurants on 5th Avenue South. The tour and history lesson continue around Cambier Park, colorful Tin City and the Bayfront area near the Depot Museum before returning to base.

The tour covers about four miles and time flies by as you tour the area at a faster speed than walking. Be prepared to stand and ride for almost two hours as part of the tour.

If you find riding the Segway addictive, you can actually buy one as Naples Segway Tours is also a local dealership. It could be a great way to get to the shops, although carrying any purchases home could be a problem!

Additional Information
Wear flat soled shoes or trainers and do not expect to carry anything with you as you need both hands for steering the Segway. There is a small zipped compartment for carrying a camera, keys and small personal items.

Admission

Two-hour tours for adults cost $74 per person, although discount coupons are available from <u>Groupon</u> and on the official Naples Segway Tour website.

Opening Times

Segway tours are offered daily at 9 a.m., noon and 2.30 p.m. Reservations are required.

Where to Eat in Naples

You will pass Tommy Bahamas restaurant on 3rd Street S as part of your tour and it's always a favorite place to dine. There is indoor and outdoor seating and the menu is a little different from the usual American fare. Try the bean dip starter and the Sanibel Stuffed Chicken entrée.

The Old Naples Pub on 13th Ave S continues the history of Naples where the tour left off. It's good for sandwiches and cold beer for lunch and is fairly priced.

Fifth Ave S also has a great choice of dining venues including the Brambles English Tea Room and Alberto's on Fifth.

Nearby Attractions
- Tin City
- Naples Depot Museum
- Palm Cottage and Norris Gardens

Naples Zoo at Caribbean Gardens

Naples Zoo is one of the top attractions in southwest Florida. Although not extensive, the 52-acre gardens are the ideal size to explore even on the hottest day. Florida black bears, zebra, lions and a collection of rare animals and reptiles can all be enjoyed in the tropical garden setting.

Naples Zoo has some very unique attractions such as feeding the giraffes and riding a camel for a small additional fee. A 20-minute boat ride takes visitors around the ape-inhabited islands. Show times, feeding times and Meet the Keeper provide information and education along with the chance to get up-close to the local inhabitants.

Picnic tables, clear signs and a Gift Shop make this a well-planned attraction for all ages.

Location

Naples Zoo is off US-41/ I-75 opposite the Coastland Center Mall.

1590 Goodlette-Frank Rd
Naples
FL 34102
Tel: (239) 262-5409

www.napleszoo.org

Things to Do at Naples Zoo

Naples Zoo is fairly small and easy to cover in a day. It is a collection of rare animals in a shady tropical garden setting with a number of large, easily recognizable animals including giraffes, zebra, lions, monkeys, big cats, alligators, gazelle, antelopes, wallabies and Florida black bears. They all have generously sized enclosures with naturalized vegetation and clear floor-to-ceiling windows for youngsters to get a good view of the more interesting animals. The bears even have a huge ice cube to scratch, drink and play with in hot weather.

The zoo also has numerous smaller creatures such as honey badgers, beautiful red and green macaws, porcupines and insects. There are plenty of relatively unknown animals and rare species too. Some of the most fascinating creatures are in the glass-fronted displays near the admission desk in the Gift Shop and they are worth looking out for. They included the mossy toad and some very unusual colored frogs and insects.

At the admission desk, visitors receive a map of the zoo and a list of timed events for the day. It is well worth earmarking some of the Meet the Keeper events and one of the Feature Shows as these are the real highlights that make this zoo so uniquely special.

The 20-minute long Feature Shows are held in the shady Safari Canyon Open-Air Theater, which has tiered seats overlooking the stage area. If you have small children the best places to sit are on the very front row, or the very back row where they can stand on the seat. There are also close-ups on large screen TVs. The shows include a lot of talking and are very informative for both adults and school children 8+. However, on my visit many families with younger children left the show early as the presentation did not hold the attention of children under school age.

The two zookeeper animators keep up a humorous and educational repartee assisted by a further zookeeper who shows the various animals to the audience. Animals in the show include a large sloth, a python, a skunk and a barn owl which flies across the arena in a beautiful silent display. The highlight during my visit was the young ocelot which actually jumped onto the keeper from one of the stands to great applause.

The admission ticket includes a 15-20 minute cruise on Lake Victoria which gives everyone a good view of the various primates, lemurs and monkeys. They all live on small islands and have plenty of ropes and trees to climb. Best of all, the animals are safely contained without any need for walls and fences. The guide gives an informative commentary about each animal and indicates points of interest along the way.

Visitors of all ages will find the giraffe-feeding a fascinating experience to either watch or take part in. For an additional fee, visitors are given several leaves of romaine lettuce to hand feed to the giraffes. One or more of the giraffe herd will be hanging over the gate and they reach down, curl their black tongue around the green leaf and eat it. This is a great photo opportunity and even young children find it absolutely thrilling and memorable.

Follow the meandering paths around and you will find plenty of picnic areas, drink vending machines and restrooms. There are also several places where you can buy drinks, snacks, ice cream and shaved ice. I found the staff members were all exceptionally friendly and talkative, from those organizing the boat trips to those serving the shaved ice. They all wanted to ensure we were enjoying our day and generally made the whole visit a real pleasure.

Another add-on attraction is riding on a camel along a dusty trail around the Cypress Hammock area of the zoo. Even if you do not participate, it is fun to watch and photograph.

Other Meet the Keeper Shows around the zoo include a talk about fosas of Madagascar, a coyote exhibit, a snake handling show, hand-feeding the alligators, a tiger event and a talk and close-up look at honey badgers, including learning how they got their name.

Additional Info

If you buy your ticket online there is a $3 discount on adult tickets and $2 off child admissions. There are no refunds, so the best tickets to pre-purchase are gift certificates and you still get the online discount. These are valid for any day, up to 12 months from the date of purchase.

Cost of Admission
Adults $19.95
Children 3-12 $10.95

Admission includes all shows and the Primate Expedition Cruise.

Cost of Additional activities:
Hand-Feed the Giraffes $5
Ride a Camel $5

Opening Times
9 a.m. to 5 p.m. daily
Closed Thanksgiving and Christmas Day

Where to Eat at Naples Zoo
The zoo has Wynn's at the Zoo Café near the entrance with a range of sandwiches, salads, snacks and drinks. At the opposite end of the zoo near the giraffe enclosure is Wynn's Jungle Café where you can enjoy a meal overlooking Lake Victoria.

There are ample picnic areas and tables in the shade for those who have brought their own picnic.

Nearby Attractions
- Naples Fifth Ave Shops and Galleries
- Naples Museum of Art
- Naples Botanical Garden

Norris Gardens Tours

One rather overlooked attraction in Naples is the guided tour of the Norris Gardens that surround Historic Palm Cottage, the HQ of the Naples Historic Society. These small, beautifully designed gardens are an interesting way to learn more about Naples' history and development.

Green-thumbed garden enthusiasts will also find the gardens are an inspiration for planting their own garden with drought-tolerant Florida plants, flowers and fruit.

Did you know that native American Indians used the toxic fruit from the Coontie to make flour, or that a banana plant must have 38 leaves before it produces fruit? It's all part of this informative guided garden tour!

Maintained by a small but dedicated team of volunteers and a regular contract crew, the gardens are immaculately maintained and always have something of interest to see, whatever the season. Whether you join a guided tour of the gardens or explore the gardens on a self-guided tour, the plants are all clearly labelled, making identification easy and informative.

Location
Located one block east of Naples Pier.

Naples Historical Society Educational Headquarters
Historic Palm Cottage
137 12th Avenue South
Naples
FL34102
Tel: (239) 261-8164

www.napleshistoricalsociety.org/norris-gardens.htm

What to Expect at the Norris Gardens

Check in at the entrance to the Historic Palm Cottage before entering the gardens with your guide through the picket gate. This is where you will get your first glimpse of the themed gardens and the waft of fragrance from the Confederate Jasmine covering the arbor, if it is in bloom.

Led by Dottie Giles, the garden tours begin in the shade beneath the open-sided Chickee. This traditional Indian hut was built by native Americans from hardy Cypress trunks and Sabal Palm thatch.

A quick introduction to Naples' history reveals that the adjacent Palm Cottage was built in 1895 for an early settler and founder of the city, Walter Newman Haldeman. The following year the Naples Hotel opened nearby, and the cottage was pressed into service during busy periods as a 7-bedroom annex for hotel guests. The nearby pier (constructed in 1888) was where guests arrived by steamboat. Their luggage and provisions were all transported to the hotel via a boardwalk that ran past the gardens.

As you drink in the lovely view of the gardens surrounding the oval zoysia grass lawn, you will learn a little about Crayton Cottage that once stood on the land now covered by these serene gardens.

The land was bought by the Naples Historical Society in 2004 to protect it from development, with the aid of a generous donation from the Norris Family Foundation, among other named benefactors. In appreciation of the family's philanthropic support in preserving Naples' history, the newly created gardens took the Norris family name when they opened in 2006.

Sheltered by the Cocoa Plum hedge, the six compact themed gardens showcase a diversity of plants, including Florida's only native palm, the Sabal, which is also the state tree. Take time to linger and look at the many names on the Patrons' Walk of those who have made these gardens possible.

The first garden on the tour is the **Pioneer Garden**. Dottie points out the drought-resistant native plants including showy flowering bromeliads, crown of thorns and the striking golden bamboo, said to have been used for the funeral pyre of native Indians. The aged Sapodilla tree was a veritable candy store, providing *chicle* from the bark for chewing gum, and chocolate/root beer flavored fruit for cooking.

The delightful **Garden of the Senses** provides scented ylang ylang blooms and waxy frangipani. Look for the bark of the Screw Pine that gives this tree its name, and explore the many other plants bordering the crushed shell path.

The **Serenity Water Garden** is indeed a place for quiet contemplation with its shady palms surrounding the lily pond. The flowing bronze sculpture of a blue heron and a kingfisher was created for the gardens by William H. Turner. If you peek through the gate from the street, the fountain sculpture is perfectly framed in the palm-tree-shaped cutaway.

The **Palm Collector's Garden** is a source of more information as the tour reveals that Florida only has one native palm—the rest are non-native settlers, a little like the city itself! Identify the Spindle Palm, the Bottle Palm, the Triangle Palm, and many more unusual species. You'll learn lots of fascinating Florida trivia on the tour, such as how the Christmas Palm and the Teddy Bear Palm got their names, and which palm can easily be identified by its crisscross leaf stems.

Pass the purple Queens Wreath climber to reach the **Edible Garden** where heritage tomatoes, herbs, peppers and citrus trees closely resemble how any garden would have looked in early Naples, mostly out of necessity. You'll see the bountiful Star Fruit Tree, green Sugar Apples dangling above your head in season, and learn that pineapples don't grow on trees.

The tour continues past the historic Guest Cottage to the spreading Sapodilla Tree. Look up to see the Cereus Cactus that mysteriously produces spectacular white blooms at midnight, which vanish by morning.

The tour ends in the **Everglades Shade Garden,** where flowering orchids flourish on the peeling red bark of the Gumbo Limbo tree. More unusual plants include an enormous white Bird-of-Paradise beneath an even larger Ficus, which apparently is still only 45 years old and still growing.

Once your tour is over, you can support the Naples Historical Society by visiting the online Gift Store, or stroll one block west to the historic Naples Pier and beach.

Additional Information

As well as the Norris Gardens Tour, Naples Historical Society offers walking tours of the Naples Historic District and other docent-guided tours of Historic Palm Cottage, Naples oldest house (1895). Details of these and other tours can all be found on the Naples Historical Society website.

Garden Tour Admission
Adults $10; Members of the Naples Historical Society and children 10 and under are free.

Opening Times

Historic Palm Cottage Museum is open Tuesday-Saturday 1 p.m. to 4 p.m.

Guided Tours of the Norris Gardens are offered every 1st and 3rd Thursdays in the month at 10 a.m. and last about 45 minutes. Advance reservations are required by calling (239) 261-8164.

Where to Eat near Norris Gardens

Fifth Avenue South has plenty of top restaurants for evening dining, but the Tulia Osteria also opens daily for lunch from 11.30 a.m. This rustic Italian restaurant has scooped many local awards with its trio of chef/owners. Delicious pizzas and salads are ideal for a light but tasty lunch while the house made pastas and entrees provide a heartier meal at very competitive prices.

Nearby Attractions
- Naples Zoo
- Naples Botanical Gardens
- Naples Segway Tours

Sanibel and Captiva Islands

Sanibel Island is the place Arthur Frommer ranked as his all-time favorite resort, even above Bali! Lying just off the coast of Fort Myers, this barrier island is a cross between Hilton Head Island and Key West, with a distinctly laid-back, casual atmosphere. It is certainly very pleasant to visit, although it can be somewhat crowded at times.

Sanibel Island is roughly 12 miles long, three miles wide at its maximum point and has an elevation of just four feet! The Sanibel-Captiva Road, Sanibel's conservation corridor, runs roughly east-west and leads over the short bridge at Blind Pass onto Captiva Island, which is just five miles long and half a mile wide.

Pastel-painted holiday homes hide amidst gardens of tropical foliage beneath shady strangler figs and palm trees. Dedicated bicycle trails run alongside the main roads making it very easy to cycle around this flat island. The beaches are undeniably gorgeous with narrow strips of white sand lapped by the azure Gulf of Mexico waters. Famous for its shelling and wildlife, thanks to the "Ding" Darling Wildlife Refuge, the island enjoys a Caribbean feel without the hills!

Location

Located 41 miles north of Naples, these barrier islands are accessible via a causeway and bridge just offshore from Fort Myers Beach.

Sanibel and Captiva Island Visitor Center
1159 Causeway Road
Sanibel
FL 33957
Tel: (239) 472-1080

http://sanibel-captiva.org/

What to Expect on Sanibel and Captiva Islands

After paying the $6 toll (oncoming only), drive along the narrow causeway past white sandy beaches lined with cars and trucks. Parking here is free and Causeway Island Park is right on the edge of the clear blue water, making it popular for those with their own beach chairs and coolers. Just offshore, bathers share the calm waters with kayaks and sea-doos. It is also a popular area for windsurfing and kite surfing. Fishing enthusiasts can be seen waist deep in the warm water and pelicans, gulls and the occasional dolphin may herald your arrival.

Once on Sanibel Island itself, there is an informative Visitor Center at the island-style Chamber of Commerce building on the right-hand side of Causeway Boulevard. It has a good supply of maps and information on cycle hire, boat trips, restaurants and accommodation.

A network of roads circumnavigates the island with a separate walking/cycle trail running alongside the main routes. One of the prettiest areas is Periwinkle Way (turn left at the four-way stop at the end of Causeway Blvd after arriving on the island). This winding road leads down to the marina and Sanibel Lighthouse, a rusty iron framework which is not particularly photogenic. However, nearby is the Lighthouse Beach Park Fishing Pier, a boardwalk nature trail and a quiet beach for beachcombing at Sanibel's easternmost point.

The short drive gives a preview of the rest of the island as drive through the Old Town neighborhood lined with small businesses. Sea grapes, scarlet-flowering poinciana trees, hibiscus and bougainvillea thrive in the tropical gardens and the undeveloped areas are covered in native greenery and cabbage palms. In the other direction, Periwinkle Way leads to San-Cap Road, the "Ding" Darling National Wildlife Refuge and the bridge to Captiva Island.

Gulf Drive, the island's other major route, runs along the southern edge of the island and is lined with resorts, beaches and homes along the water's edge. Small parking lots are reserved for residents with permit stickers and lead down to the private residents' beaches.

Apart from the Wildlife Refuge, most of the eastern end of Sanibel Island is built out with villas and holiday homes, some grand and palatial with long private driveways, while others are more typical beach houses painted in aquamarine, sky blue or primrose yellow. Many of the properties are used as small hotels or B&Bs with the occasional real estate office, surf shop, café or olde worlde inn. Sandy paths lead down to the beach giving access for local residents and there are glimpses of swamp in the less developed center of the island.

Most people visit Sanibel to enjoy the beaches which are worthy of any Caribbean island. As much of the waterfront is developed, visitors are limited to the public parking areas with beach access. Parking is strictly monitored, so make sure you display your parking ticket ($2 per hour) prominently before heading for the beach.

Bowman's Beach
The main beach is Bowman's Beach, a long stretch of white sand reached by a 5-minute walk from the car park over a wooden bridge spanning the creek and mangroves. This secluded beach has soft white sand strewn with thousands of seashells. It shelves more steeply towards the sea and high tide is marked by a bank of shells, one of the main attractions of Sanibel Island.

This undeveloped beach rarely feels crowded and visitors can be seen performing the "Sanibel Stoop" as they walk along the shoreline picking up all types of shells from twisted whelks to rose pink tellins. The beach is also a haven for wildlife with nesting birds and sea turtles often seen here.

J.N. "Ding" Darling National Wildlife Refuge

Almost half of Sanibel Island is protected by various wildlife refuges. The "Ding" Darling National Wildlife Refuge is the largest, covering more than 6,000 acres. It was established in 1976 in memory of the Pulitzer award-winning cartoonist and conservationist J.N. "Ding" Darling and it protects one of the largest undeveloped mangroves systems in the USA. Located just off the San-Cap Road, it has its own car park and Visitor Center.

Visitors can walk, cycle, kayak or drive on the four-mile Wildlife Drive through the refuge or take a ride on one of the eco-friendly trolley tours with an experienced guide. The refuge is home to 250 species of birds, 30 types of mammals and 50 types of reptiles and amphibians.

Captiva Island

Sanibel's smaller sister, Captiva, can only be reached by boat or along the Sanibel-Captiva Road which runs along the center of Sanibel Island and over the bridge at scenic Blind Pass. Turner Beach at Blind Pass is one of the two public beaches on this quiet island and is known for its excellent shelling.

Captiva warrants just a single road, appropriately named Captiva Drive and there are no cycle paths, making it more hazardous for riders. On one side of the road are large vacation homes, condos and restaurants while on the other side there are uninterrupted sea views with small private footpaths running over the dunes to the long stretch of private white sandy beach.

Once you reach Chadwick Square with its cluster of small shops and the Post Office, the remainder of the island is privately owned by South Seas Resort. There is parking and public beach access at the end of Captiva Drive at the Alison Hagerup Beach Park, near Chadwick's Square.

Additional Attractions on Sanibel

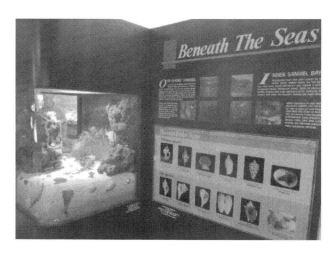

Bailey-Matthews Shell Museum

Those with a fascination for pretty seashells will enjoy a visit to the informative Bailey-Matthews Shell Museum on the San-Cap Road.

Sanibel-Captiva Conservation Foundation (SCCF)

Located at Mile Marker 1 on San-Cap Road, this attraction has walking trails, an observation tower, butterfly house, aquariums and a marine touch tank. It offers educational programs about its research and wildlife preservation programs.

Clinic for Rehabilitation of Wildlife (CROW)

This 42-year old clinic welcomes visitors to its Healing Winds Visitor Education Center. It offers educational talks, hands-on exhibits and critter-cams to watch recovering patients.

Admission

Sanibel Causeway Toll $6 per vehicle
Entrance to Bailey-Matthews Shell Museum $11 for adults, concessions for children
"Ding" Darling Refuge Wildlife Drive $5 per vehicle; $1 per walker or cyclist
Entrance to CROW $7 for adults, concessions for children
Entrance to SCCF $5 for adults, free for children under 17

Where to Eat on Sanibel and Captiva Islands

There are a host of places to eat on both islands to suit all budgets. Bailey's on Periwinkle Way has outdoor dining along with a bakery, hot/cold deli and coffee bar as well as a restaurant. Beachfront casual dining is offered at Traditions on the Beach inside the Historic Island Inn on W. Gulf Drive, Sanibel.

There are several good waterfront restaurants on Captiva Island. Try the Mucky Duck at the end of Andy Rosse Lane or the Green Flash Restaurant on Captiva Drive for informal waterfront dining.

Nearby Attractions

- Downtown Fort Myers (See my book "Days Out Around Fort Myers")
- Edison-Ford Winter Estates (See my book "Days Out Around Fort Myers")
- Clam Pass Beach and Boardwalk

Scenic Drive - Everglades City, Ave Maria and Immokalee

This scenic drive connects some of Collier County's largest and oldest communities. Along the journey there are museums, airboat attractions, state parks, wildlife refuges, hiking trails, visitor centers, citrus groves, boardwalks, shops and restaurants for you to stop and visit as you please.

The total driving distance including all detours is 137 miles, but the route can also be completed in stages, returning directly to Naples at several points. Allow 3 hours driving time to complete the circuit, plus stops at various attractions and museums. Some of the highlights along the journey, including Collier County's Museum of the

Everglades and the Audubon Corkscrew Swamp Sanctuary, have their own chapters with full details.

Enjoy the drive, take your camera, stop for refreshments and discover the real Florida-in-the-raw on this wonderful road trip.

Location
Circular 137-mile drive around the highlights of Collier County.

www.avemaria.com

www.colliermuseums.com/locations/immokalee_pioneer_museum

What to See on this Scenic Drive
Your scenic drive begins by heading south/east from Naples on Hwy-90/US 41 (Tamiami Trail) towards Miami. After 33 miles, turn right on SR-29, signposted Everglades City. You will see the Everglades Chamber of Commerce Information Center on the junction.

Just three miles down the 29 is Everglades City, a quiet sleepy city with dozens of motels, B&Bs, villas, lodges and hotels. Boards along the road advertise airboats, kayaking, fishing and adventure tours in this Everglades outpost. It's well worth turning up and taking an airboat tour. They run hourly from several departure points along the waterfront of the Barron River or on Lake Placid which both flow into Chokoloskee Bay.

Continue down Copeland Ave to the historic city center with City Hall now occupying the 1928 Old Collier County Courthouse building.

Everglades City was the first seat of Collier County, which was established in 1923. Nearby is the white clapboard building of the Everglades Community Church with its impressive Westminster chimes marking each hour. Turn right on Broadway Ave and park beside the lovely pink building that now houses the Museum of the Everglades. It is well worth a visit and is described in detail in a separate chapter.

If you continue along Copeland Ave you will pass many stilted homes, the airport offering 10,000 Islands Air Tours, several boat/airboat tours, an observation tower and a wildlife boardwalk.

Big Cypress Swamp National Preserve Welcome Center.

Retrace your route back along SR-29 to the Tamiami Trail (US-41). If you want to make a detour,. just 4 miles east of SR-29 on the Tamiami Trail (US-41) is the Big Cypress Swamp National Preserve Welcome Center. There are always huge gators lying on the banks of the slough which can easily be seen from the boardwalk. The welcome center has some excellent exhibits and information about the wildlife on the Everglades and shows an interesting film about the swamp and its resources.

From the US-41 junction with SR-29, head north along the edge of the Big Cypress Preserve through Copeland. The scenery is varied with dense fir trees giving way to more typical Florida greenery including palms, pine forests and Spanish-moss draped cypress.

Florida Panther National Wildlife Refuge

The high metal fencing indicates the boundary of the Florida Panther National Wildlife Refuge, a 26,000 acre natural sanctuary to protect the habitat of the endangered Florida panther (only 80-100 remaining). Other threatened wildlife including Everglades mink, Florida black bears, wood storks, limpkins, indigo snakes, orchids and rare fox squirrels also thrive in the area. There are signs for hiking trails in the reserve during daylight hours.

Further north you will pass orange groves which are heady with the scent of orange blossom in spring. The groves are laden with orange fruits from December onwards when the packing and distribution centers are working flat out. Further north, cattle grazing and agriculture are in evidence.

Ave Maria

About 28 miles north of the US41/29 junction, look for Oil Well Road on the left, signposted for Ave Maria. After about 5.5 miles you will arrive at the grand entrance to one of Florida's newest cities, Ave Maria, founded in 2007.

The winding paved road runs for 3 miles and is beautifully landscaped with flower beds. It is bordered with hedges beyond which you will see agricultural land and tractors busy producing fruit, tomatoes and vegetables for Collier Farm and its seasonal Farm Shop.

The city of Ave Maria is still being developed with luxury homes on residential estates by Del Webb, Maple Ridge and Pulte Homes. There is also a golf course, town center shops, supermarket, Ave Maria Catholic University and schools.

The city is centered on the Ave Maria Oratory, a contemporary church with an exposed steel structure. The impressive façade depicts the Archangel Gabriel greeting the Virgin Mary with the words "Ave Maria" after which the city is named. The 30-foot high white relief is carved from Carrera marble sourced from the same quarry in Italy used by Michelangelo. The exterior of the church is built from contrasting orange/dark brown stonework with gold statues of the 12 apostles in alcoves above the entrance.

It's worth taking a short tour inside the church where you may find choirs rehearsing or organ music playing. The main features are the plaques over the doorways and the organ on the balcony.

The church is surrounded by a circle of small businesses, cafés, an ice cream parlor, pub, jewelry and gift shops selling mainly religious artworks, icons and relics. The area is very quiet and peaceful; ideal for sitting outside and enjoying a meal or refreshments.

Immokalee

Return to Oil Well Road and take the next left turn (Camp Keais Road). This joins highway CR-846 which ends in the center of Immokalee in 8 miles. Turn left on SR-29 and after a sharp right-hand bend you will see the Immokalee Pioneer Museum on the right.

This sizeable town is Collier County's largest inland community with many churches, banks, fast food outlets and local businesses lining SR-29. The name "Immokalee" is the Seminole word for "my home" and it has been home to a variety of settlers including Indian traders, trappers,

Gillian Birch

cattle crackers, farmers, hunters and missionaries since it was settled in 1873.

Immokalee Pioneer Museum

The Immokalee Pioneer Museum at Roberts Ranch is a 15-acre living history museum with free admission. Once the home of the Roberts family, it was the longest running ranch in South Florida.

The land now has a collection of pioneer homesteads and preserved farm buildings which can be explored, each with its own information board. The relocated buildings depict life on a pioneer homestead and citrus grove in the early 1900s.

Highlights of this open-air museum include the beautiful two-story Ranch House, built in 1926 for the Roberts family who donated the house and land to Collier County to create the museum. There's a 1930s Bunkhouse for laborers and the Hide House where hides were salted to preserve them before they were shipped to Raiford prison where inmates worked in the tannery.

The Horse Barn and Seminole Chickee provide further insight into life in early Florida while the restored Cane Mill was used to press cane juice which was then boiled in a kettle for syrup. The museum site also includes the First Baptist Church which was built in 1928 for $616.

Immokalee - Naples

Immokalee is a good place to enjoy refreshments and a walk around the local shops before returning to Naples along the CR-846 (back towards Ave Maria). The road winds for 30 miles through the rural countryside, passing the entrance to the Audubon Corkscrew Swamp Sanctuary (see separate chapter) before reaching the I-75 (Exit 111).

You can return to Naples by heading south for 6 miles to exit 105 on the I-75 then follow the Golden Gate Parkway (SR-886) west. Alternatively, stay on CR-846 Immokalee Road until you reach US-41 in North Naples. To the right is the famous Pewter Mug restaurant, while turning left will take you back to Naples along the Tamiami Trail.

Additional Information

Immokalee Pioneer Museum at Roberts Ranch
1215 Roberts Ave
Immokalee
FL32142
(239) 658-2466
Open Mon-Fri 9 a.m. to 4 p.m. with free admission

www.colliermuseums.com/locations/immokalee_pioneer_museum

Where to Eat on your Scenic Drive

There are several waterfront restaurants in Everglades City. They are listed in detail in the chapter on the Museum of the Everglades.

The Pub and Grill in Ave Maria is a friendly Sports Bar with an extensive menu covering basic lite bites, lunchtime burgers and sandwiches and a traditional dinner menu of pasta, meatloaf and stir-fries to complement the all-day menu of salads, tacos and fish 'n' chips. There is also a Tropical Smoothie Café and several other eateries around the Annunciation Circle.

Mi Ranchito and Kountry Kitchen are two of the most popular restaurants in Immokalee, or save yourself for a delectable Prime Rib dinner at the well-established Pewter Mug in North Naples on the journey home.

Nearby Attractions

- Everglade City Airboat Tours
- Big Cypress Swamp National Preserve Welcome Center

Tin City

Located on the waterfront, Tin City was the birthplace of Old Naples. The tin roofed structures of these former warehouses and docks have been repurposed to house an eclectic collection of independent shops, cafés and boat tours with a distinctive maritime feel.

Mostly under air, this abstract collection of shabby-chic 1920s buildings provides just the right amount of character. Stroll around the small shops, enjoying glimpses of the old waterfront docks and fishing boats from the boardwalk and open-air tables of two waterfront restaurants.

It's definitely an authentic Naples experience you will not want to miss.

Location

Located one block south of Tamiami Trail, off 9th Street South

Tin City Shops
1200 5th Avenue South
Naples
FL34102
Tel: (239) 262-4200

www.tin-city.com

What to Expect on a Visit to Tin City

Parking is plentiful around the Tin City complex, or you can reach it as part of the hop-on, hop-off Naples Trolley Tour. Most of the shops are in a series of seven renovated warehouse buildings which are connected along paved "streets". Wander through the fascinating complex of independent stores selling jewelry, fashion clothing, beachwear, gifts, bags, art and home accessories.

More unusual businesses include tropical wine tasting at the Naples Winery store and delicious sweet treats at the Monkey Bread Factory. Their pull-apart cinnamon caramel buns are divine accompanied by a gourmet coffee from their Espresso Bar.

The atmosphere captures the feel of Old Florida as you explore what's on offer in over 30 local businesses within this unique undercover shopping complex. The open wooden rafters, old barrels, giant ship's wheel, fishing nets and old rails and workings all add to the historic charm. Quiet background music and the hum of conversation makes this a great place for browsing, shopping and dining at a relaxed pace.

Outside, the businesses continue along the boardwalk overlooking the Gordon River. Here you'll find a flotilla of fishing and pleasure boats, including the sightseeing catamaran and flotilla of Pure Naples tour boats.

Where to Eat at Tin City

There are several places to eat at Tin City, but for people-watching it's hard to beat the central location of M&Ms Café. Friendly service and a wide menu of burgers, sandwiches and wraps make this a popular hangout for local shop owners as well as visiting tourists. The tempting offer of free samples of homemade ice cream lure people to try some of the 28 flavors on offer, piled onto Cinnamon Vanilla Waffle Cones that are made from scratch at the café.

Pinchers Crab Shack has an extensive menu of local fish, seafood and other favorites with some outdoor tables overlooking the river. This local restaurant chain is famous for its stone crabs and fried fish, best enjoyed in Tin City's authentic waterfront setting.

Alternatively, the Riverwalk is an authentic fish house in Tin City. The nautically-themed restaurant serves great food at indoor and outdoor tables overlooking the river.

Admission
Free

Shops Opening Times
Open Monday – Saturday 10 a.m. to 9 p.m. (Restaurants generally until 10 p.m.)

Sundays noon – 5 p.m. (Restaurants 11 a.m. to 11 p.m.)

Nearby Attractions
- Naples Botanical Garden
- Naples Depot Museum

OTHER TITLES

Look out for more books by Gillian Birch in this popular series:

- Days Out in Central Florida from The Villages

- Favorite Days Out in Central Florida from The Villages Residents

- Days Out from The Villages with Grandkids

- Days Out Around Orlando

- Days Out Around Fort Myers

- Days Out Around Clearwater & St Pete Beach

- Days Out Around Cocoa Beach

- 20 Best Florida Beaches and Coastal Cities (Also available in color)

- 20 Best Historic Homes in Florida(Also available in color)

COMING SOON

- Days Out Around Miami

- Days Out Around Orlando with Children

- Days Out in Central Florida for Active Seniors

- Days Out Around Sarasota and Bradenton

- Days Out Around Venice

- 20 Best Gardens in Florida

These will all be available shortly in paperback and ebook format. Keep up with future publications at: www.gillianbirch.com

ABOUT THE AUTHOR

Gillian Birch is a freelance travel writer and part-time Florida resident. As the wife of a Master Mariner, she has traveled extensively and lived in some exotic locations all over the world, including Europe, the Far East and the Republic of Panama. Her love of writing led her to keep detailed journals which are a valuable source of eye-witness information for her many published magazine articles and destination reviews.

Describing herself as having "endless itchy feet and an insatiable wanderlust," she continues to explore Florida and further afield, writing about her experiences with wonderful clarity and attention to detail.

Gillian has a Diploma from the British College of Journalism and is proud to be a member of the International Travel Writers' Alliance and the Gulf Coast Writers' Association.

**

If you enjoyed this book of Days Out Around Naples and would like to recommend it to others, please consider POSTING A SHORT REVIEW on Amazon or on your favorite book review site.

Your honest opinion is truly appreciated by the author and helps other readers to judge the book fairly before buying it.

Thank you so much!

42823576R00071

Made in the USA
San Bernardino, CA
09 December 2016